Poetic Voices 2008

Edited by Claire Tupholme

YoungWriters
First published in Great Britain in 2008 by:
Young Writers
Remus House
Coltsfoot Drive
Woodston
Peterborough
PE2 9JX
Telephone: 01733 890066
Website: www.youngwriters.co.uk

SB ISBN 978-1 84431 784 4

Foreword

Young Writers was established in 1990 and has been passionately devoted to the promotion of reading and writing in children and young adults ever since. The quest continues today. Young Writers remains as committed to the nurturing of poetic and literary talent as ever.

This year's Young Writers competition has proven as vibrant and dynamic as ever and we are delighted to present a showcase of the best poetry from across the UK and in some cases overseas. Each poem has been selected from a wealth of entries.

Once again, we have been supremely impressed by the overall quality of the entries we have received. The imagination, energy and creativity which has gone into each young writer's entry made choosing the poems a challenging and often difficult but ultimately hugely rewarding task - the general high standard of the work submitted ensured this opportunity to bring their poetry to a larger appreciative audience.

We sincerely hope you are pleased with this final collection and that you will enjoy *Poetic Voices 2008* for many years to come.

`Contents

The Poems

Help

Help, I'm drowning in a sea,
A sea of never-ending hopelessness.
Sorrow cannot explain
All the terror and the pain.

Will anybody rescue me?
My rage is large,
My upset is deep.

I shall run beyond the hills.
I find myself trapped,
All hope abandoned,
All happiness gone.

My face is exposed to a friendly face,
I'm rescued.

Leah Murphy (12)

Untitled

It's cold outside,
The winter is here,
Santa comes in days.
The snow is falling, soft and white as clouds,
Children's laughter echoes as they play,
Spreading happiness and joy yet again.

Yellow is the colour of spring,
Newborn lambs gambolling,
Chicks are chirping in their nests,
Bunnies bouncing through the fields,
Daisy meadows all around,
The smell of spring is in the air.

Oh! How I love the summer sun,
White sand and lovely beaches,
Playing games and having fun,
Ice cream melting,
A dip in the pool,
A trip to the spa,
Endless days, according to Mum.

Crunchy autumn leaves,
Red, orange and gold,
The sound of rakes across the ground,
Jumping! Skipping through piles of leaves,
Oh, the joy!
The sound of children laughing,
All over the blue skies,
Can't wait for the fun to begin again.

Iona Montgomery (9)

Portrait Of A Miser

As friendless as a fly in a spider's web.
Secretive, quiet, shy. As lonely as a lost child.

Scrooge is as wrinkled as a screwed-up piece of paper,
Creased and withered as if he is knocking on Death's door.

He is greedy, grudging and green-eyed.
He is as selfish as a sinner.

You can't help but notice Scrooge's mean,
Ungenerous, envious, sly face,
Looking as harsh as a strict teacher.

Standing alone as sour as a lemon,
Furtive, solitary, bitter is Scrooge.

As sharp as a piece of flint.
Skin, ghostly, pale white.

He is as rough as sandpaper.
A miser is Scrooge.

Georgia Strachan (12)

Without You

No one to hug me when I am down
No one to act with me like a clown
No one to share with me that special secret
No one to trust so they can keep it
No one to get into trouble with after Geo
No one to get fashion tips out of the magazine 'Cleo'
No one to sleep next to underneath the tree
Then to be told you will never know what you mean to me.

No one to swim with in the backyard pool
No one to try out new sweaters when it gets cool
No one to text to in the middle of the night
No one to understand how my coffee has to be just right
No one with whom I can have a secret handshake
No one to go out with for a milkshake
I know I do not say it constantly
But you really do mean a great deal to me.

You are the person who calms me down
You always make sure I have no frown
I know you will find the driest joke funny
And drag me out of bed to watch 'Bugs Bunny'
It is sad that I seldom see
That you are part of me
You are my best friend and my sister
And I write this poem to let you know
That I will never let our friendship go.

Elizabeth Tugwete (13)

Let Us Forget

Let us forget that we live in an empty world
Where people don't know what they are looking for
And they drift around like clouds in a dull grey sky
Searching for some kind of colour.

Let us forget that we live in a blind world
Where no one sees the lost child in the supermarket
And the bleeding fox lies dying by the roadside
Waiting for the clock to stop ticking.

Let us forget that we live in a silent world
Where no one can hear the trees screaming
And the crisp packets are blown around like leaves
Moving like underwater swimmers.

Let us forget we live in a lonely world
Where there are no presents under the Christmas tree
And the old woman sits alone by the fire
Hoping that her doorbell will ring.

Let us remember that we live in hopeful world
Where the sun shines through the rain
And there is one man who holds the door open for the next
Smiling as he says, 'good morning'.

Kerry Nesbitt (15)

French Camp 2K7

F antastic views
R aining but still fun
E xciting activities and walks
N ice food
C oming together as a team!
H aving fun

C ollecting information
A greeing with each other!
M aking new friends
P laying together.

Emma Barrett (13)

Hit And Run

My best friend is sixteen years old
There were so many that we said and told
But the day they stole her, it broke my heart
Our worlds were split and torn apart
It was a normal day and I remember it well
When the car hit her and she fell
I stood still, not moving an inch
I couldn't help but just stay and flinch.

I rushed on over to her side
Her eyes were closed but her head was open wide
The people who did this have taken my best mate
I tried to save her, and knew I was too late
I called for help and waited by
But there was nothing I could do but try
The ambulance arrived, and took her away
I stayed with her and only prayed

We reached the hospital, and they took her through the doors
I sat and waited, I felt like I was in a war
The nurse came through, and said they couldn't start her heart
My world now felt empty, and like I was torn apart
I went on home, with her on my mind
The things I saw that day have made me blind
I laid my head softly on my pillow
I wept and wept, I felt like a whomping willow.
Falling asleep, I wish I was with her
But just remembering how things were
I fall asleep, my heart feels torn
I have nothing left to live for
I hold onto her jacket, made of leather
Falling asleep, and now thinking of her lying in the heavens . . .

Karen Boswell (15)

Spirit Friends

Spirits walked beside me,
All the way to town,
Even though the clouds were out,
And the sun was down.

When I moved, so did they,
They copied every turn,
And when I could not see the way,
Their glowing light did burn.

But soon, alas, they were called home,
Away into the sky,
To stay and guard the sleeping souls,
And watch the world go by.

Alice Keel (15)

Midnight Horse

Sneaking through the midnight hours,
Up the hill, heading for the towers
Where my pony as magical as can be,
Is waiting somewhere up there for me,
Ducking low, I tear my shirt,
'Oh no, oh quick! Poachers alert!'
I hear a bang and then I fall,
Desperately I begin to crawl.
By now I am all covered in dirt,
I'm soaking and wet but luckily not hurt.
I hear the footsteps treading behind,
Horrible thoughts, running through my mind.
Tears are pouring down my face,
As I get up, and begin to race.
I'm desperately seeking my magical dream,
We are a friendship, we are a team,
I stumble and fall face down, I get hit.
Standing above me, my wonderful Spirit.
Snorting and kneeling I grab onto his mane.
And galloping through the trees and back down the lane.
Hugging him closely I close my eyes,
My friends would just call him a bunch of lies,
As I lie in bed and think of him,
Until tonight my friend when the light is dim.

Cassandra Eades (11)

Illusionary World

Like trees, hills and valleys
Tall, high and low
The greens, the misty and the vegetatives
Seen everywhere you go.

Tall, high and low
The poor, the rich, the middle
Loitering in beauty, rags and unsatisfied though,
With wealth, peace and prosperity to kindle
The poor, the rich and middle
The rags, bronze and gold
Seen wherever you paddle
Living like the days are old
The rag, the bronze, the gold,
Living down below our hills
Ah! The rag, the bronze, the gold
Tears, confusion and feary joy seeking pills
Living down below our hills
This funny illusionary world
Of shattering isolated hills
Dying, killing and fading.
Why? We are not told
This funny illusionary world
Where rags and bronze punish gold
Gun avenging in daylight bold
Yet can never transform into the gold
Where rags and bronze punish gold
To give life an insipid sweet taste
In vain all they do to help the gold
For the Lord God controls their haste.

Obigho Lucky Akhenemhen (18)

Bad Weather

(A poem for my mum)

Now things are changing
a sigh means more than
I want, I want, I want
a sigh is the starting of a storm -
I wish, I wish, I wish . . .

I watch her tired troubled eyes
but cannot reflect their sorrow.
They are mirrors for the place
that I will never see.
A place so different – so confused,
not even helped by my
encouraging, hopeful
smile.

She sits silent, scared perhaps
and spoons her food into her speechless lips
that don't know what to do.
I stare, hopeless, at her idle hand
stirring her cold pasta
round and round
and remember when I was young -
she fed me with the flying jets
and chugging trains.
I would laugh and shout for more

But now I don't know what to do.
I don't think any transport would
get her anywhere.
I'll just wait.
I'll be here until the storm subsides.
Oh I wish, I wish, I wish . . .

Claire Ewbank (15)

Alfie, The Brother From Hell

My little brother, my best friend,
He is a freak and a fool, to the end,
He's locked in his room, smokes forty a day,
How the hell can he live that way.

I try to help him out, he is a prat,
He draws on my pictures and stuff like that,
Little brother I do it because I care,
You beat me up, attack me and pull my hair.

I want you to get a job,
So you don't have to live like a slob,
Little brother Alfie, I love you,
Regardless of how and what you do.

Years have passed, Alfie has changed,
He will always be weird and strange,
Now I don't have to put up with him, this is why,
I watch over him from the sky.

In case you wonder and want to know,
I collapsed in Alfie's room a long time ago,
He was the reason for my death,
Because of him I drew my last breath.

Teri Manning (15)

Gatekeeper Of Emotions

I'm walking through a sea of fire,
If I let my emotions rule me the consequences could be dire,
I'm as cold as ice,
I no longer believe in being nice,
Your words like a sword slash my heart,
I will end this story as you gave it a start,
Oh God why don't you state,
What's written in my fate?
Why must you string me along?
In my head I repeat over and over the same sad song,
Hate is my weapon,
Destruction is my need,
You made me what I am today,
You planted the hatred seed,
The wrath of my fury you will fear,
Your cry of distress is what I want to hear,
You played with my emotions as though it was a game,
You weren't concerned with who you hurt,
As long as you kept your 'good name'
To hide from me this world is too small,
I will catch you before you fall,
You wanted me now here I am,
You knew you did me wrong,
But you didn't give a damn,
Never oppress someone so that they are forced to rebel,
They can turn your life into a living hell,
When I look at you I feel disgusted,
You're one of those people that can never be trusted,
Reality grips me and forces me to check in,
I know hurting someone is a sin,
In the Almighty I do trust,
To believe in His power is a must,
He will do for me what needs to be done,
My faith is my sword,
And my words are my shield,
I believe in the Almighty, He will level the playing field.

Farah Ali (19)

Footprints In The Snow

I walk half frozen with my papa
Hand in hand my footsteps in sync with his.

Just us talking. From time to
Time me running ahead, on the powdered land.

Thoughts gather, spill,
Break the silence of the misted air.

His loose grip breaks, now
And then. As if he's trying to flee.

Looking back on this scene,
My mother explained, was the day he left me.

I look back upon our trail,
Where the lane meets the new road.

Every time the winter comes
I can still see the footsteps left in the snow.

Scott Wilson (14)

Death

I can walk yet my feet are planted.
    I feel the shadow yet the light is blinding.
My youth but a young bud plucked before its prime.
    My wiring of nature but a cruel twist of fate.
The lark has sung yet the nightingales still call.
    I am suspended yet I cease to fall.

My tolling of the bell is but a christening of the grave.
    Life accomplishments are but an unravelling ribbon.
Unstressed and yet stressed.
    No sunlight hereafter and yet hopes of some white serenity.
My flowing craft is but a crawl.
    I am suspended yet I cease to fall.

Catherine Dwyer (15)

Another Rainy Day

Sitting on my window sill
To escape from here is my only will
Staring through the pane of glass
Hoping my last day will pass.

I can't stand the shouting anymore
The pain she's caused reminds me of war
How much longer must I live this way?
Deprived of happiness and freedom each day.

I lie awake all through the night
Am I strong enough to win this fight?
There is no hope for a girl like me
She destroyed my future, can't you see?

How could she want to hurt her own kid?
The scar on my back says what she did
I'll never forget what she has done
A confused, weak child is what I've become.

Louisa Sadler (14)

Clyde's Great Aunt Claire

'Why do I have to visit Great Aunt Claire?
She moans and she mutters and she has no hair.'
'What a load of nonsense!' my mother replied
'She's a really sweet lady, on the inside.'
'Yes, but it's the outside I have to see
She does nothing but knit and drink milky tea.'
'Yes, well we're here now at the old people's home,' my mother said
'You don't have to talk to her, just sit on her bed
Off to her room now, number six six five
And do behave now, my Clyde.'
I stuck out my tongue and walked to her room
I knocked on the door, *boom boom boom*
'Come in' came my great Aunt's tone
And inside I went to a great big moan
'Not you again,' she said with a sigh
'Oh my goodness, what a day this'll be, my oh my
You bore me to death, you do my young Clyde
You're rude, obnoxious and just a tad snide
I cannot bear your visits to me
Oh! Get out of my sight and fetch my tea
Find the matron inside the kitchen room
And say that I sent you
Once you have done that chore
I want you to do a few more
Collect my washing, it's in a white bag
Inside is a pair of knickers and a cleaning rag.'
So off I went, brought her the things
Organised her watches, necklaces and rings
Remade her bed, a whole seven times
And recited to her a truckload of rhymes
I dusted her bath ducks (why, I don't know)
And finally, it was time to go home
Mother said, 'Ah, I bet you and Claire are now the best of friends!'
I laughed at the thought, not if the *world* ends!
I never want to see that woman again!

Emily Clarkson (13)

How To Make A Good Penguin

How to make a good penguin
He needs . . .
Ears as invisible as air
Yellow stomach like gold
Feathers like velvet
Beak as sharp as dagger
That's how to make a
Good penguin.

Iain Chambers (12)

Our Time, Appleby

Mam is sewing, the stock must be ready in time,
Blue, lemon, knickerbockers sublime.

Sitting in the room, daylight till dark, material everywhere!
A worried look comes over tired eyes.
Will they sell or won't they?
She has to make it pay.
Cleaning to do, tea to prepare, as only she can.

I love me bit o' Mam.

Me and my sister, excited to go, shopping to do, outfits to buy,
We've got our own style to shout.
Daring to think that we may be asked out!

The vardos (wagons) are ready: we're all tingling with joy.
The water, food, chitty irons and a big pot or two.
'Brother have you put the bedding in?'
'Me little sis we have it all,' he looks up with a grin!

Here we go, Dad getting the rest spots ready.

Could Bella go another mile or would that be too far?
She trots the flats, gallops the high, she's excited too, woe girl, steady.

Soon she will be washed and tethered on green grass by a river,
In due course.
At the side of a lay-by, Bella is a 'good old horse'.

I know that people driving by, will look at us and stare,
But what will they see?
A yog (fire) and age old traditions that have been for centuries.

I love my roots, my life, but most of all, I love my Romany family.

Victoria Lee (13)

Happy Birthday?

I find a box in my room,
Containing a pile of memories
That will never be anything more.
At the bottom, I see a photograph
Of those carefree days
When we were young.
I let my mind wander
Back to the days
When we were young.

There we are. At the party
All smiling our false photo smiles.
Who smiles like that?
Really?
Some of us are posing.
Big, unnatural poses.
Fake poses.
The sort of poses
You only have for parties.

The birthday girl sits on our shoulders,
Looking down upon us,
Like a queen gazes down,
Upon her adoring subjects.
Our nails freshly painted,
Painted by the professionals,
Who came and went.
Us wearing the sort of clothes
You only wear for parties.

Some of us lean forward.
Some of us lean back,
To make sure everyone is seen.
Others,
Block the view,
Of another at the back,
With their hair.
The sort of hairstyle
You only have for parties.

There I am,
At the end.
At the front,
Almost smallest,
When we all stand straight.
Holding the tattered head
Of the dead piñata.
Bernard Frederico,
I named him.

He was my mascot for the evening.
Had to have him in the picture,
I joked.
They took me seriously.
His stripes were loud.
Bright and colourful.
Blues, pinks, oranges.
Strange colours
For a paper donkey.

It was funny to think,
That a moment ago,
He was tortured.
Tortured by us.
Stuffed with candy
Until we murdered him.
Beat him with sticks.
For sweets.
Happy birthday?

Zoë Fletcher (13)

Elemental Love

It began like air
As I would float
Among clouds.
You swept me off my feet
As I flew
On wings of love.
Hopes and dreams
For our future entwined
Lifted high by the winds
Of ambition.

Flowing like water
Our bond progressed,
Breaking the banks
Of our expectations.
Your rain calmed me down
Yet you were an ocean;
Unpredictable, exciting
I thirsted
For more.

Passion grew like fire
In the heat of our romance,
Where ruled by desire
We kissed.
It sparked an attraction
Of a different kind,
As fuelled with lust
We burned our innocence -
Our two flames merging
As one.

As an echo on the breeze
Your love faded,
Leaving only emptiness
And bitter cold.

My river of tears
Cleansed me of love,
As I drowned in the torrent
Of loss.

Heated arguments,
Tempers rising.
Your insults scorched
Like flame.

Gone with the wind,
Washed away with the tide,
Our relationship burnt out
And died.

Claire Chambers (16)

My White Labrador Called Tia

My white Labrador called Tia
Can sometimes be a pain,
When we try to tell her off
She thinks it is a game.

Whether she's inside or outside,
She eats everything she sees.
Then when she gets tired
She'll lay down and go to sleep!

When we first got Tia,
She was 2 months in years.
At first she did make some young kids,
Burst out in tears,
This was, of course, accidental as Tia is harmless as can be,
In fact, Tia is one of the most harmless dogs,
You're ever going to meet!

When she gets excited,
She'll pee all over the floor.
Then you'll wish you went a bit faster at opening the door.

I love having a dog around,
They're so much fun.
But I'm glad I don't have to clean up after her,
That's a job for my mum!

Paul Shuster (14)

Over The Top Boys

The rats and the mud flow down the way
They're all running as if to say
Don't go with them you know it's bad
Fight your fears and stay here lad

The ladder stands tall in front of me
Waiting for men to climb to see
The bullets, the fire, the trees, the dead
The men would rather stay here instead

The whistle is blown, the screams and roar
The horrific pictures from this war
The lads go down just like dominoes
My friends, my mates, my enemies, my foes

The sounds of death freeze me still
My legs they dare not move they fear the kill
The bullets fly past left and right
The horror continues into the night

I sit alone in a puddle of mud
Surrounded by body parts, guts and blood
Only one thought goes on through my head
The thought of all my friends now dead

General Haig what have you done?
You kill us freely as if you've won
You sweep us up as if we're toys
With the haunting sound, 'Over the top boys.'

Tom Fleming (16)

Flawed

There's a crack in the lens of my camera.
So much for those Kodak moments.

No one wants to see broken landscapes
where the earth cracks at the centre or
photos of families that were once whole, intact -
now flawed by that darn line in my lens.

I could of course replace the lens
have a new one shaped precisely for my camera;
a replica processed
by the hands of those who have moulded thousands of identical
lenses . . .

Stupid idea, really.
Though my lens is cracked, it's still unique, for I have shaped it myself.

Look Mummy! I did it all by myself!
I have shaped it myself.

Screw perfect images.
They can keep their Kodak moments.
My lens may be slightly flawed, but my camera is still whole
and in fine condition.
And who knows -
maybe if I replace its batteries someday
I might take more positive pictures.

Claire Helfrich (19)

Silent Killer

You see them there, in the corner,
They've already crossed the border,
The invisible line,
The step that could kill
And strangely enough
It is by their own will.

The smoke, it creeps out through their lips
And harms their bodies bit by bit,
Lives are being shortened,
Lungs slowly choking,
They've been told before,
But they think we're joking.

They think it's cool, they think it's smart,
But it is tearing them apart,
Lighters ignite again,
As more victims fall,
For the deadly ride,
As they follow its call.

As soon as it starts, hard to end
And all the damage, hard to mend,
The kids, they don't listen,
They just find it fun,
They do not realise
The damage being done.

Adults though, they can be to blame,
They are also in this foul game,
Where did addiction start?
Will it ever end?
Before you know it,
You've joined the deadly trend.

Hollie Strong (13)

Confusion

Confusion is just like a knot,
Too hard to untie till the day it rots,
It makes it hard to know where you're going
And it sets the seeds of anger glowing.
Confusion's to be head over heels,
But to love; a very different feel,
Not to know if you are in or out,
Just makes me want to scream and shout.

Joe Savage (12)

The Unlucky Monkey

Once a monkey tried to reach a tree ahead
But a coconut fell on his head.

After he tried to jump a river
But instead he fell in the deep river.

In a circus they made him jump through a hoop of fire
But he burnt himself with a burning wire.

William Giagu (8)

Dolphins

A tail wagger
A smooth swimmer
A fish hunter
A high leaper
A large jumper
A deep diver
A quick swimmer
An eye gleamer
A scaly diver
A sneaky catcher
A small hunter
A swift pouncer
A crab watcher
A deep thinker
A speaky caller.

Bethany Greenwood (9)

Hallowe'en

The twisted trees
As black as coal
The fog drifts in
Like a long-lost soul
The blackened woods
Where bats do play
They hunt at night
Then rest all day
The gravel path
With stone graves either side
The castle's pitch-black
And the door's brown and wide
From the highest tower
Comes a sudden scream
Strange things happen
On Hallowe'en.

Madison Howard (14)

The Wind In My Garden

The wind is blowing everywhere
My garden is bare
But I don't really care

The wind is blowing everywhere
It's blowing me away
Over the hills and over the hay
Bye, bye you won't see me today

I wish it would be nice and sunny
So I can go outside and play with my mummy

I wish I could move to a different place
So I can always have a nice face

But it's never going to be nice
I am always getting bored
Just want it to be a nice sunny day
But I am always in my bedroom
Lay, lay, always lay
Every day.

Stacey Bierley (13)

A Goldfish Tale

Swimming around my little bag, waiting for a new home
Swimming around my little bag, feeling scared and alone
Swimming around my little bag, a hand reaches for me
Swimming around my little bag, I will no longer be lonely
Swimming around my little bag, a new family has been found
Swimming around my little bag, I'm dropped, I hit the ground
Gasping for breath in my broken bag, waiting for someone to
Help me
Hanging on for life in my broken bag, a man bends down to
See me
Frightened and helpless in my broken bag, he walks away
Shaking his head
I'm left dying in my broken bag, knowing nobody cares
If I'm dead.

Sophie Walker (14)

USA Poem

At 12 o'clock the towers fell,
I heard the news and had to tell.
At 12 o'clock the word got out.
And people started to shout.

We had time to run away,
Well until the end of day.
Time began to fly,
People began to say goodbye.

The people that did the crime
Have caused people a very sad time.
Families are falling apart
The people that did this don't have a heart.

September 11th is a very sad day,
We wanted to help so we started to pray.
We will always remember this very sad day,
Please make the families happy again.

Jemma Evans (15)

Change

Nothing lasts forever
People come and go
They stay a while
Make you so happy
Then it changes
And leaves you sad.

If only I could go back
Stop the change
And spare my feelings
Make them stay
Make the happy moments last
But everything changes

Does nobody else see
That change isn't always good
Impermanence
The worst word
If only it wasn't true.

Rebecca Fitchett (13)

Sorry!

It was just a normal autumn day, I was hanging the washing out
I put the last thing on the line then I heard a shout
'Kirsty', came the voice which I knew I could not ignore
It was the voice of Edith Jackson the lady who lives next door

I knew something was up by the expression on her face
'Your grandad's been rushed into hospital!' my heart began to race
I automatically rang my dad as I didn't know what to do
He quickly returned from football so we could go and visit you.

I tried my very best to see you every day
I stopped with Nanna most of the time to make sure she's okay
I went on Tuesday evening you were looking better than ever
I said farewell and see you on Thursday as I was
Goin' town tomorrow . . .
Depending on the weather.

I ended up goin' to town and stopped with Nanna that night
As early Thursday was goin' with Nanna to
See if you were alright
I awoke to the sound of ringing, 'will someone answer the phone
It was when there was no reply I realised I was alone.
I hesitated for a moment then I picked it up
It was my Aunty Michelle, I already knew what was up.

I looked out of the window, the ground was getting wetter
It couldn't be my grandad, he was getting so much better
As time passed on and clouds started to clear
I heard the door handle someone was here
My dad looked round the door but he was not alone
I realised at this point my grandad wasn't coming home!

I've cried you a river Grandad, I feel so full of pain
Because I made you a promise but then I never came
I have so many memories some are good and bad
You never knew I loved you although I always had
So I'm gonna have to end this I just want you to know
I'm sorry I didn't see you before you had to go
I love you so much Grandad I know it's a little late
But be watching over me Grandad and be waiting at the gate.

Kirsty Dawson (15)

Mass Destruction

Destruction, destruction everywhere
It makes me want to stare,
How could this place
Once filled with peace,
Just cease to now be
Nothing more than a memory.

Despair, despair everywhere
Just an old boot and a mangled pear,
All the woodland creatures,
Left to die
In the beds they lie
For it came and left
As quick as a flash
Like the blink of an eyelash.

But it did not stop
Or be merciful,
The mess it left was plentiful,
A great big monster
Gleaming red, orange and yellow,
But leaving black
Where it had mellowed.
The sadness it can leave
You cannot believe,
For fires cause mass destruction
Everywhere.

Beth Shuttleworth (13)

Mrs Autumn

She walks through the clear sunny days,
Spreading her colourful joy.
Her beautiful, long flowing rustic dress,
Harmonizing with her ruby red vibrant hair,
Entwined with magnificent, blossoming flowers
Laden in fiery oranges and thriving greens.
Walking towards the faded gold grass,
That had once been summer green.
As seasons change, she must change too.
Life's adventure.

Noticing the animals preparing for colder days,
They scurry and scamper searching for food
Brown acorns, delicious nuts and juicy, wild berries.
She would miss all the animals
The squirrels, rabbits and foxes.
Tears rapidly began to fall.
Autumn rain.

Trees begin to lose their russet, golden leaves,
And they crunch under her feet.
She has garlands of onions and carrots upon her slim neck,
Wreaths of wheat and barley were used as a belt.
The earthly smell of fruit and vegetables clung to the air,
The wet dampness smelt of gorgeous perfumes.
Kindly she spreads her last sunlight to help the end of the harvest,
For golden apples, delicious oats and tasteful pomegranates.

Brassy brown and fiery orange foliage lay upon the ground.
The colours fade in beautiful decay,
The frosted, dew covered spiderwebs lay glistening in the darkness.
She places them on her pale neck.
Her once glorious gown is becoming black and colourless.
She does not want to accept the cold days to come.
Anger rages through her and she spreads her thunderous emotions,
The sunny days are gone

All Hallows Eve.
The trees are bare and colourless, yet stand strong and tall.
Coldness spreads across the land,
Bitter, whistling winds sound like crying in the night,
Spreading evil and sorrow.
Spirits for her past come back to haunt her,
Taunting her for her days will end soon.
A ghastly mask is upon her face and clothes are torn and dirty.
A jack-o'-lantern is used to scare away the ghouls and ghosts before the darker days.
it is time to accept the days to come,
Remember the past,
And embrace the future.

Colours explode around her,
Magnificent greens, pinks, blues and silvers race across the night,
Like rainbows in the sky,
Whizzing and zooming towards the heavens.
A great bonfire is burning before her,
She steps timidly towards it,
The final step in a lifelong journey,
Throwing away the magnificent jewels and colourful clothing,
She watches the burning embers fade.
And realises that this is not the end but a new beginning.

Julie Dobbin (13)

Summer To Autumn

Summer is a wonderful season, you can
Enjoy yourself, have fun without reason.
Swimming and holidays are best
Theme parks, water parks and the rest!
Remember to have lots of fun, keep safe
And now my story of summer
Is officially *done.*

As the season changes we now creep into
Autumn as the trees whisper to one another
Autumn is nearly here.
Howling winds showering crisp, gold leaves
To the damp muddy floor
Deer grazing on the cold misty mornings.

Hedgehogs gathering ruby red leaves,
To snuggle down for the winter
Air looping in the sky,
River trickling down the stones.

Ryan Compton (13)

It's A Cat's Life

In the garden is where we play,
And laze around in the sun all day.
We chase the birds, the bees and mice,
Although they don't taste too nice.
I go in to get my tummy tickled,
And play and get into a pickle.
I have my dinner when I'm hungry,
It stops my tummy from going rumbly.
I live with my mummy and my sister too,
My dad had to go because he weed on a shoe.
My owner is sweet and gives me cuddles,
And laughs and smiles when I jump in puddles.
I sleep on a rug in front of the fire,
There really couldn't be anything else a cat could desire.

Tamsin Dean (14)

My Wish

My wish is to say how I feel about issues surrounding us,
Instead of cars, why not catch a public transport like a bus,
Or recycle paper instead of throwing them away;
I know everyone has something that they have to say.

My wish is to meet the music band, Tokio Hotel, of my dreams,
They make me want to achieve more because that's how it seems,
Their lyrics have meanings that make you think twice,
If I ever meet them, I know they would be ever so nice.

My wish is to be honest and truthful with everything,
It will be hard to lie and say a rabbit can sing,
But in the fairy tales, the goodies always win,
That's because they say the truth instead of committing a sin.

My wish is to stop all kinds and forms of bullying,
So mankind can live in peace and harmony without suffering,
There are people being bullied now and need to stop,
Bullies are horrible and they cause a teardrop.

My wish is to travel the whole entire world for fun,
I like to discover, eat, shop and give it a run,
There are so many places out there that are fantastic,
I could visit every place at the point of a finger click.

My wish is to achieve the goals and faith of my religion,
Islam is my desire that I will never want to darken,
Every step I take I learn and become more peaceful.
All I want is to be a good person and become faithful.

My wish is to live my life to the best possible standard,
And have the greatest possible moments as I have preferred,
If there is an opportunity that I cannot miss, I will go for it,
So my wish is to be the best I can be and don't miss a single bit.

Thamanna Khan (14)

As A Teen

As a teen I find it really sad,
There's never any good news,
Concerning us it's only bad,
The media paint us in a bad light,
It isn't all, it's just a few,
So it's unfair and not right,
When I'm out with my brother,
He's not even one,
So they think I'm his mother,
People look at me in disgust,
Or throw me dirty looks,
It's unfair and unjust,
We have a bad reputation,
But there are some good,
Teens in this nation.

Chloe Harrison (14)

Internal Hardship

Never fear the walk away
Life was always tough
The hateful things that people say
Sometimes it's all too much.

When the world turns black
And your soul's exposed
You feel the heat from Hell, it's rising
Your life is gone it's never coming back.

Hope has abandoned what you stand for
When you fear you've reached the end
When all you want is the warmth of love
To the flaming pits you'll descend.

The barren wastes of loneliness
The cold is creeping in
The Hell-bound executioner
Will make you pay for every sin.

The shattered shards of faith
Lay melting at your feet
The tempered hammer of insecurities
It's swift and yet discreet.

When no one wants to listen
And no one understands
When you've wandered through the shadows
Find the light within my hands.

Daniel Tattersall (15)

August 1914

Do you remember the street we used to walk on,
The fluent breeze,
The soothing heat of the setting sun,
The early songs of birds,
The morning tram, its greeting
emptiness to early risers of the morn;
Let stillness speak,
No need for words
when comfort in silence is sought . . .
(and found?)
Have you ever experienced freedom-
the kind that uplifts, that gives you
wings when standing at the edge of cliffs;
when following the winding slopes of hills,
when running through a
boundless field of wheat . . .
(of heaps to reap?)
The sun-dried stalks caressing your skin,
crickets coquetting with your ears-
Stop. Listen. The larks fly low
this August day; remember what hazy
days await, unwarranted today.

Natalya Mykhaylyuk (15)

This Is What I See

I see you as my true love to be,
I see your heart's love is deep,
We get along well
No fights, no nothing,
This is what I see.

I see you as a shining star,
Lighting up the night,
Guiding me through all my troubles
Wow, you shine so bright.
This is what I see.

I see my courage strengthen,
It grows, grows and grows,
But when I see you go,
I'm just a girl standing alone.
This is what I see.

I see you as a boy,
Who understands others,
Who has a gift to understand,
You, me and others.
This is what I see.

I see myself smile,
As you walk through the gates,
You make others happy,
And you think of me as a mate.
This is what I see.

I see you as my closest mate,
But my boyfriend one out of eight,
When you look, touch or talk to me,
It feels like you grab my heart.
This is what I see.

I see you're like no other,
You are very unique,
No one can please me,
But my love is what I seek.
This is what I see.

I see a boy in front of me,
Standing with your mates,
Someone laughing, someone smiling,
This is the one for me.
This is what I see.

I see you walking to me,
Sad and gloomy as if you're sorry,
You told me you were moving to America,
My spirit drooped low.
This is what I see.

I see you once every two years,
I miss you so much,
Goodbye my love.
This is what I saw.

Joelle Littlejohn (13)

The Golden Eagle

Our golden eagle is a magnificent bird,
He is brave and soars to untold heights.
With much ease, it glides through the sky,
So that no adversary could catch him
Even if they tried.

With distant eyes,
The golden eagle flies majestically
Through the skies.
With its tawny wings that spread out wide,
We can see its mightiness in its eyes.

The golden eagle is such a good flier,
Its strength other birds desire.
He never takes a rest,
That is why he will always be the best.

If a prey is not cautious,
Eagles will be vicious.
As eagles love to devour,
With much pleasure almost every hour.

The golden eagle is such a hero to
L W Young,
Like this great bird, our spirit will never
Be outdone
It inspires us in our lives to succeed,
In sports, academic quizzes and
Spelling bees.

When L W Young is put through any test,
We will always try to do our best.
With great strength, vision and grace,
We'll soar to win every race.

Daffyd Ameeral

Lying In Mam's Bed Again

Lying in Mam's bed again
Feeling very ill
Mam and Dad think I have a virus
Because I have taken every pill

Lying in Mam's bed again
Aches and pains everywhere
Covers over my head
Cuddling my teddy bear

I am feeling much better now
The virus has gone away
I really hope it doesn't come back
Any other day!

Stephanie Williamson (10)

Mummy

Our mummy is so beautiful
Her hair is so fine,
She treats me the way she treats my sister
She is most wonderfully kind

She does my hair for school
The knots are all out carefully,
She takes us out to fun places
And she cuddles us when films are scary.

She is on her hands and knees
24 hours a day,
We tell her to sit down and rest
She doesn't listen to what we say.

At the end of the day, she shares her love
With me and my sister too,
She kisses us at night-time
And our teddies too.

Hayley Schofield & Hannah Schofield (11)

The Snow

The snow has filled the ground,
It's special scent filling the air,
It's wonderful, just wonderfully cold,
Its pure white colour,
I can never take my eyes off
Its admiral sound of silence is so loud
Snow . . .

Delaram Imantalab Kordmahaleh (9)

Alligator's Pain

Free from the world, the great alligators roam
Living in a swampy, greeny home
Away from humanity, away from fear
Everyone knows its dangerous here.

What a great dream, for alligators
Especially when you're in the circus
Beaten and battered the alligator cries
Tearful, sorrowful, no cheerful eyes.

Whipping, whacking, it is not right
How would you feel if you were whipped all night
Made fun of, and laughed at,
Tortured to put on funny hats?

He was always the king of the swamp,
Anyone entered they would die with a chomp
Brave like a lion, strong like a giant
Now he is dead he lives happy instead.

Brandon Chambers (11)

African Child

African child born in the wild
Loved by the ones who see you.
Sleep while your mother guides your dreams into the light.
More children walk down to the water well faster than the
Tears of others who wait for their return.
My little one shall come back to me
And I shall hold him in my arms.
His skin like mud, his hands like pebbles
And he will slowly drift away.
Some day my little one shall not walk one mile with me
To get one cup of milk or water to drink.
He shall sleep while his papa earns enough money to feed us.
My little one is only two years old
And yet he has walked so long,
He might not make it to eight years.
His small delicate feet worn out, like leaves floating to the ground.
One day my little one's leaves will fall
And he will drift away to a world of darkness.
I love my little one.

Isobel Corrie (9)

Sadness

Roses are red,
Violets are blue,
I'm so sad,
Are you sad too?
Don't brighten my day
With pink petals
Or a walk across the bay.
Just leave me to sob
Or drop onto the water
Where my tears lay.

Emma Cullen (9)

On The Day I Was Born!

The sky was pink and blue,
Not a single cloud to be seen.
The sea was shimmering over the sand.
The trees still and calm.
Rivers rippling as boats ran through them.
Birds singing and whistling a tune.
The wind flowing gently through the park.
Flowers blooming uncontrollably,
Their perfume sweet and lush.
Planets spinning around the burning sun.
The world beneath my feet.

Lucy Freeman (13)

I Am

I am what I am
I am what you see
I carry a bag of gravity
I am what I am
I am what you see
''Cause I'm so big
I'm floating in space
Because I am Earth.

Veronica Faluyi (9)

Love

Love is a hot blood red.
Love sounds like loud heartbeats.
Love looks like a beautiful red apple.
Love feels like a red rainbow shape.
Love smells of perfume.
Love reminds me of happy times.

Tyler Talmadge (8)

The Ballad Of John Lennon

He's getting old
And can't get hold of life,
Like a penknife
Slipping away from his hand.

Born in Liverpool
A lonely boy,
His name was John
He had no joy.

To his aunt he went
Until he was old,
Bought him a guitar
That he thought was gold.

Went to a school
Called Quarry Bank,
He met some friends
Then called themselves,
The Quarry Men.

The Quarry Men
Still in school,
Changed their names
To The Beatles.

Had an audition
Which they failed,
All their life
Was like hail.

Just kept trying,
Not even crying
Until they found a manager.

The Beatles became famed,
Now they're not ashamed!

Jesse Ira Abadilla (9)
Grove Park Community School, Sittingbourne

School Holiday

Clocks tick backwards,
Manikins dance,
French books wish
They were in France.

Paint brushes
Fall on the floor,
And colouring pencils
Start to draw.

Cupboards open
Then slam shut,
Paper screams,
As it is cut.

Mice try to break free
Of their wires,
Fire alarms yell
As they smell fires.

Glue-sticks glue
The books together,
Grass would like
A change of weather!

Oliver Mattinson (11)
Ramsbury Primary School, Ramsbury

I Like To See . . .

I like to see . . .

Birds hopping around
in the morning sunshine.

Big, white snowflakes
falling onto the soft white ground.

The twilight sky
after the beautiful sunset.

The twinkling sea
where the fish like to swim.

I don't like to see . . .

Raindrops falling from the sky all day,
animals that are dying.

Cruelty to animals and children,
my friends crying . . .

Rebecca Womersley (10)
Ramsbury Primary School, Ramsbury

Six Things Found Under A Goose's Wing

Two ends of a never-ending rainbow.
The beak of a parrot lost many years ago.
A bag of stars from an unknown galaxy.

A golden tree stolen from clouds up above.
The longest stripe off a zebra's coat.
A silver feather that will never lose its shine.

Hannah Fox (11)
Ramsbury Primary School, Ramsbury

Five Things Found In A Fairy's Bag

The biggest pearl found in the ocean
filled with cries of the sea.
A phoenix's feather plucked by the Queen.
The most precious unicorn horn.
A pair of butterfly wings and a pot of fairy dust
made from a pure crystal white star.
A magical tree made from the wood in the secret garden
at the edge of the world.

Georgia Ghent (11)
Ramsbury Primary School, Ramsbury

I Like To See . . .

Christmas presents standing solemnly under the tree,
A dog trudging through an overgrown park,
A small baby grins for the first time,
And a swallow dives through the sky.
An author sitting in silence wondering what to scribble next,
The smell of popcorn wafting through the air,
And natives dancing through a peaceful forest.
New life being revealed,
A cave being excavated
And someone finding a four-leaf clover.

Marnie George (11)
Ramsbury Primary School, Ramsbury

I Like To See . . .

I like to see . . .

The red roses swaying in the breeze,
The reflection of a rainbow shimmering in a lake,
A duckling taking its first step and then falling over,
A baby rabbit bonding with its mum.

I don't like to see . . .

A baby lamb dying of heart break,
A four-year-old crying because she has fallen over,
A bully taking a child's lunch money,
A baby finch that has lost his mum.

Emily Rodriguez-Martin (11)
Ramsbury Primary School, Ramsbury

One, Two, Three . . .

One odd ostrich obstructed offensive omelettes,
Two tricky ticks tickled the tempted Tinkerbell,
Three tiny tigers taught table tennis to toilet trained tadpoles,
Four flying fish fired flames for freedom,
Five flaming falcons fought five flamingos,
Six stupid snakes sacked some sceptic stags,
Seven silly sealions sailed on silent seas,
Eight eager elephants egged every educated eel,
Nine naughty nits nibbled nicotine near newsagents,
Ten triumphant turtles trekked to the tall temple.

Joseph Smith (11)
Ramsbury Primary School, Ramsbury

Playtime

Hooray! The bell rings.
Playtime!
Football, here we come!

The open grey tarmac,
Ready for Cristiano Ronaldo hopefuls.
Coloured cones stand to attention,
Marking the boundaries.

Play starts.
Like a yo-yo
The ball goes back and forth,
Back and forth,
Finally a *goal!*

Oh no!
The final whistle.
Game over,
Lining up time,
Back to work.

Jack White (11)
Ramsbury Primary School, Ramsbury

I Would Like To . . .

I would like to ride on the back of a ferocious lion,
to find the end of a rainbow
and to fly with a golden eagle.

I would like to swim down to the lowest point of the ocean,
to touch the sizzling sun
and fly to Jupiter with the birds.

I would like to go back to World War I in a time machine,
to hear the steps of a caterpillar
and to pick a fiery feather from a blackbird.

I would like to beat a cheetah in a race,
to find another solar system
and to hear a snail thinking.

Alex Tellwright (11)
Ramsbury Primary School, Ramsbury

Likes And Dislikes

Things I like to see.

I like to see animals leaping in the playground.
I like to see bunnies playing joyfully in a yellow meadow.
I like to see the sunset reflecting on the ocean.
I like to see butterflies flying in the air.
I like to hear peace in the air.

Things I don't like to see.

I don't like to see dogs lying covered in blood.
I don't like to see the night because bad things happen.
I don't like to see people die in war.
I don't like to see animals hunted.
I don't like to see children screaming.

Freddie Swain (11)
Ramsbury Primary School, Ramsbury

I Would Like To . . .

I would like to hear the step of a ladybird
And hear the thoughts of my dog.
I would like to touch the beam of the sun
And fly with a phoenix.
I would like to fly on a dragon
And dive to the centre of the Earth.

I would like to run as fast as a cheetah
And be as slimy as a slug.
I would like to travel the universe
And find the end of a rainbow.
I would like to walk across the sea,
And bottle the first word of a newborn baby.

William Hine (11)
Ramsbury Primary School, Ramsbury

Summer, Winter At Sea

In the summer the sea relaxes in a hot tub,
The boat slowly strolls along the top of the sea,
Feeling content, the sun smiles over the world.
The moon watches the ocean with a cat's beady eyes.

Winter comes and the waves jump up like a tiger pouncing on its prey,
Waves, rain and wind bully the boat, pushing it to and fro,
The wind whistles through the sails making it chilly.
Lightning winks a flash of light, and then it's over . . .

Jack Steen (11)
Ramsbury Primary School, Ramsbury

A Number Poem

One obese orang-utan organises orphans,
Two timid tigers terrorise Tom,
Three talented tabbies travel to Thailand,
Four flamboyant foxes fight for fire,
Five famished frogs fly,
Six selfish seals secretly shoot Sophie,
Seven septic spiders sever shoes,
Eight electrocuted elks educate effervescent elephants,
Nine neutered newts nag Norman,
Ten tortured turtles taste tequila.

Jonny Budd (11)
Ramsbury Primary School, Ramsbury

During The Holiday

Chairs are playing leapfrog and doing the hopscotch,
Two computers playing games
Are wishing for some change,
Thinking maybe if they try,
They'll pop up in Ukraine!
One lovesick table, is sitting in a corner
Shuffling its feet about and thinking what to do.
Thank you to the phones,
(They thought it was quite funny).
The Prime Minister now does think
The head mistress is a bunny!

Sophie Goodrich (11)
Ramsbury Primary School, Ramsbury

I Like To See . . .

The penguins waddling across the Antarctic making new friends.
Paul Robinson score a hat-trick against Arsenal
In the Champion's League final.
A million pound cheque strolling into my arms.
Gordon Brown tripping up into the muddiest puddle.
The biggest wave in the world jam-packed with surfers
Testing their boards to the highest limits.
The shell of the golden, shiny sun falling down to the ground.

I don't like to see . . .

Bad news in the newspaper,
Litter on the floor being dropped by people,
Whales being hunted,
Bullies bullying younger children.

Owen Davies (11)
Ramsbury Primary School, Ramsbury

Counting Animals

One old owl owned oblongs,
Two toads tried tripping Tom,
Three thorny devils thrashed Tim,
Four flamingos flew forwards,
Five flew for fur,
Six snow leopards slew Saxons,
Seven salamanders slew sharks,
Eight eagles ate earthworms,
Nine naughty newts never knew Ned,
Ten turtles tore Tim terribly.

Daniel Cullen (10)
Ramsbury Primary School, Ramsbury

The Weather

Spring is looking for a friend
Summer's round the bend
Water's getting very clear
Baby lambs stop to spring; summer's nearly here

Summer's feeling very warm
Very kind when even dawn
Day is almost minuscule
And night is getting very tall

Autumn's raindrops are feeling cool
And also rather cold
An orange leaf is drinking beer
Autumn's shivering; winter's near

Now winter says, 'Come here Hail,
Make up a humungous gale.'
Snow is laughing with the cold
And Frosty Snowman says, 'I'm old!'

Jasmine Banovic
Ramsbury Primary School, Ramsbury

Love Is . . .

Love is the shape of a dove.
Love is the colour of green grass.
Love is the feel of a rabbit.
Love is the sound of the wind.
Love is the sight of the sky.
Love is God's creation of life.

James Melville (9)
St Ninian's Primary School, Livingston

Love Is . . .

Love is the colour of a brown Twix.
Love is the shape of a squiggly heart.
Love is the sound of the wind howling.

Andrew Barclay
St Ninian's Primary School, Livingston

Scotland

S cotland is a nice place to stay
C aledonia is our home
O range skies are in the sky in the winter
T he land has lovely colours in the fields
L ovely locations in Scotland
A ll the lochs, like Loch Ness, are really nice
N ever dive to see the Loch Ness monster
D estiny stone stolen by English.

Craig Docherty (9)
St Ninian's Primary School, Livingston

What Is A Dinosaur?

Dinosaurs are gentle giants walking in forgotten times.
Dinosaurs are big and small
Dinosaurs are deadly, scaly monsters
Dinosaurs are huge carnivores
Dinosaurs are sea dwellers flapping with their slimy flippers
Dinosaurs are rulers of the sky
Dinosaurs are my fierce friends.

John Heaney (9)
St Ninian's Primary School, Livingston

Scotland

S cottish seas are not so warm
C lyde running through Glasgow
O ut in the cold the bagpipers play
T histles are sore
L ost in Edinburgh, the crowded place
A nice place to be is in Livingston
N essie lives in Loch Ness
D own in the Almond is a good place to be.

Keanu Sneddon (9)
St Ninian's Primary School, Livingston

Butterfly Oh Butterfly

You're beautiful and light,
Up with the birds and down with the grass,
Searching for flowers in the land.
After they're done, they go out and have some fun
And lie in the sun till the day is done.
At night they go out to fly over the riverbanks.
They shine so bright, it will hurt your eyes.
They search for food, then they store up their food.
Butterfly, butterfly, goodbye!

Mariam Arif (8)
St Ninian's Primary School, Livingston

Spring

S pring is fun.
P eople take their babies to see the baby animals.
R abbits start to come out and hop in the grass.
I go out to play on my bike in the spring.
N ights get shorter.
G rass grows every day.

Taylor Paterson (7)
St Ninian's Primary School, Livingston

Spring

S pring is wonderful.
P retty flowers grow in spring.
R oots grow under the ground.
I n spring baby animals are born.
N ights get shorter and days are longer.
G rass grows in spring.

Leona Dalglish (7)
St Ninian's Primary School, Livingston

Spring

S pring is fun.
P retty tulips come out.
R abbits hop about in the woods.
I go out to play on my rollerblades.
N ights get shorter.
G rass starts to grow.

Michael Wards (8)
St Ninian's Primary School, Livingston

Spring

S pring is a warm season.
P eople play outside on bikes.
R abbits hop around.
I n spring people wear shorts and T-shirts.
N ight-time gets shorter.
G rass grows back.

Amy Bowman (7)
St Ninian's Primary School, Livingston

Spring

S pring is a joyful season.
P laying spinning on the green grass.
R ain falls more in April.
I t becomes much warmer and sunny.
N ew baby animals are born in spring.
G ardening is good in spring.

Julia Targett
St Ninian's Primary School, Livingston

Spring

S pring is fun.
P eople take their children to see the baby animals.
R abbits are hopping in the fields.
I n spring pretty flowers blossom.
N ights are shorter.
G rass grows in the springtime.

Jack Wason (8)
St Ninian's Primary School, Livingston

Spring

S pring is fun.
P eople take their babies to see the animals.
R abbits are hopping in the field.
I go out to play with my friends.
N ights become shorter.
G rass grows.

James Stewart (8)
St Ninian's Primary School, Livingston

Spring

S pring is fun.
P eople play on their bikes.
R ain helps the grass grow.
I wear shorts and T-shirts.
N ight-time gets shorter.
G rass gets eaten by the baby animals.

Harry McIlhone (8)
St Ninian's Primary School, Livingston

Spring

S pring is lots of fun.
P eople look after baby lambs.
R oots of tulips and daffodils grow.
I n spring we see baby animals.
N ight-time is shorter and it gets lighter.
G rass grows very long.

Melissa Hyndman (8)
St Ninian's Primary School, Livingston

Spring

S pring is brilliant.
P eople go swimming every day.
R oots of tulips and daffodils begin to grow.
I n spring baby animals are born.
N ights get shorter and days get longer.
G rass grows every day.

Megan Aird
St Ninian's Primary School, Livingston

Parks

Parks, parks, fun and games,
Parks, parks, slides and swings.
On the park there's a roundabout
And frames that tire you out.

Max Watson (8)
St Vincent's RC Primary School, Rochdale

Pirates

P eg-legged pirates, walking on one pegged leg.
I nvisible ignored pirates on one pegged leg
R avenous pirates fighting for fierce fish
A ngry pirates trying to chop off your head
T ired pirates on two pegged legs
E nviable pirates trying to eat fierce fish
S hiny swords and two pegged legs, scare you to death.

Harry Stockton-Smith (7)
St Vincent's RC Primary School, Rochdale

Animal Of Light

Trees stand as tall as giants,
Moonlight streaming through the leaves,
A pair of devilish eyes glares at the vulnerable village,
That crouches in the bed of the eerie wood.

Its emerald tongue, as sharp as a knife ferociously flashing
in the dead of night.
Slyly slithering towards the unsuspecting victims of the
ancient dwelling.

Ruby-red eyes glow, captivating the villagers
Luring them through breathtaking mist towards its mysterious lair.

As silent as a mouse, the slimy creature pierces its first victim
with deadly venom;
Because of the evil, a haunting scream penetrates the silence.

Horrific hurt!

Rebecca Pass, Helen Toward, Emily Clark & Abigail Potter
Sacred Heart RC School, Redcar

Animal Of Light

Wings flapping; feathers flashing,
Its frantic form, blazes the sky,
Gliding in the moonlight glow,
Stealthy movements; snow is lashing,
Eyes a preying antenna:
Scanning for its next victim.

Screeking and screeching,
Crying and weeping,
These are the sounds
That throng through the village,
Depriving people of their sleeping.

Painstakingly seeking like a pirate for gold,
Its polluted breath, repulsive and old,
Battered and smashed but still never hurt,
Twisting and diving, covered in dirt.

From first acquaintance, he may seem fowl,
You appear to be wrong,
Because this my friend, is the majestic owl.

Craig McCann, Josh Enderwick & Billy Hodgson (13)
Sacred Heart RC School, Redcar

Animal Of Light

Caring to some but cruel to others,
Animal of light.
Appears by dusk but not by dawn,
Animal of light.
A star in the sinister sky at night,
Animal of light.
It takes away your breath.

Slimy or smooth?
Animal of light.
Fair or fierce?
Animal of light.
Help or hurt?
Animal of light.
Tall or tiny?

Gives a glow like the sun on the world,
Animal of light.
A group of flashing fairy lights,
Animal of light.
Will take the shadow of sadness away from your life,
Animal of light
Because of its existence, we do not know.

Lives in a bush,
Animal of light.
Comes out at night,
Animal of light.
Screams for attention like a child,
Animal of light
Look out for this mysterious creature!

Emily Wilson (13)
Sacred Heart RC School, Redcar

Animal Of Light

In the beginning everything was normal,
Everything was calm.
The only sound made was the wind in the trees
But then . . . a perfect purr came out.
Like a snail in a race, he walked slowly forward to an open hatch
As innocent as anything to drink the milk that was there.
Towards the milk he bowed elegantly and gracefully
But he didn't know the change that was about to happen!

As fast as a blink the flashing light had gone,
The glow across the baby-blue sky,
Scattered in all directions, it sped rapidly away.
The first change had happened, it went from good to bad,
It changed all so suddenly, it changed ever so quickly.
The thing stood there all evil and still it
Began to walk forward
To the darkness that was approaching.

The ghastly beast advanced forward,
The people that were watching were in shock from surprise.
The animal took their breath away,
Because all they could see before them
Was a hairball full of evil, all black and deadly
And eyes as red as the Devil's glaring out.
The thing stared straight past them as it began to run
Its legs scratching and piercing the air and into a bush.

Katie Gordon & Megan Finlay (13)
Sacred Heart RC School, Redcar

Animal Of Light

Prowling, the noxious nefarious lion
Sends a shudder down my spine
The rotting corpses start to climb
Filling the world with doubt and dread
All mortals appear dead.

Living in the grassy plains
Inflicting hurt on all mankind
Because he's possessed in the mind
Taking in an untamed breath
Hunting souls to their death.

Flashing through the arid blades
Leaving behind an onyx glow
Creation becoming his only foe
His sinister mane casts a shadow upon
Covering all and everything's gone.

Charlie Whitfield & Danny Jones
Sacred Heart RC School, Redcar

The Animal Of Light

It elegantly flows through the stabbing blades of grass,
While the weeds loiter among the barren field,
Where the blood-curdling smell of the animals gives off
a nauseous gas,
The glow of the skin repels the stench like a steel shield.

Slithering and sliding, it nestles among the eerie ebony soil,
It breathes profusely like a lion after chasing its condemned prey,
Sticking its tongue out, it licks the trickling oil,
Standing at the side of the road perplexed, it's nearly the end of day.

As night-time falls, its devious soul enters the congested town,
The flashing stars in the sky are diamonds glistening among the moon,
Because the jet-black sky reflects them down,
The morning sun plays a mellow tune.

Walking through the arid dirt,
Sneaking through every precarious cut,
As the sun boils with explosive hurt,
It lies there with its starry eyes shut.

Sam Hitchen (12) & Jack Exley (13)
Sacred Heart RC School, Redcar

Animal Of Light

Slithering through the barren plain,
Sliming across the arid ground.
A gasp of breath; a white flame,
The cornfield turf; not a sound.

Tongue like a dagger,
Piercing its prey,
Emerald green skin
Camouflaged it shall lay.

Eyes flashing fiercely,
Coiling round the trees,
Because of its desire,
Any creature it will seize.

Bones strong as steel,
Can never be hurt.
But inside its heart glows,
No longer as dirt.

Molly Piggott & Sophie Widdowson
Sacred Heart RC School, Redcar

Animal Of Light

In the morning light,
Within the eerie swamp,
The powerful beast awakens from a sleep
of horror.
It emerges from the ominous pit,
From which it came from,
Only still to find more flesh to devour
From the innocent bug-like people,
To the eye of the creature

The wretched beast loomed over the
morning hills,
Slowly it drifts towards the minute town,
Covering every morsel of land
With hatred and sin.
Gathering victims, only still wanting more . . .

Joel Cox & Jake Gallacher
Sacred Heart RC School, Redcar

Animal Of Light

They had seen it all before;
The suffering, the violence,
The bloodshed.
The quakes indicate it coming.

Far inside the Acropolis,
Deep inside a passageway
It lies,
A vile fiend of no identity.

Inside a lair of pure sin
Compacted with large spikes and flame,
The child of the Devil awaits
Its malignant emotions to burst
As a sea of fury,
Leading the single, scintillating eye
To the site of its deadly siege.

In an outburst of flashing fury;
With a wingspan three metres long,
It soars
Out of the temple; towards the people
It scorches the air during flight.

Its bloodthirsty mind explodes
With anticipation at the thought:
Fresh victims.
Their scent flowing through the air.

The satanic beast's screech
Pierces fragile souls;
The legs like machines
Forcing the fearsome monster forward.
Teeth like scissors to cut,
And claws like daggers to stab
A Godless glow from the eye.

Closer, closer, closer,
It tears through the darkness;
A knife through flesh.
Radiates the star-filled sky.

Breath was taken from the village that night,
Blood was spilt and bones were scattered;
Tears formed an ocean.
Helpless, useless, hopeless . . .one by one they fell.

The people of the village drowned,
Swirling in rapids of torture;
The current ripping dear emotions
From their limp, lifeless bodies,
It catapults extinguishing light.
Because of the havoc,
Nothing but hurt is left.

Ross Tanfield (13) & David Russo (12)
Sacred Heart RC School, Redcar

Animal Of Light: Catastrophic

As you stare into space,
Terror evolves around your face,
Knowing that your end is near,
Your heart begins to pound with fear.

The ruby red eyes appear,
And to your horror you suddenly hear,
A piercing screech from beyond the hill,
Catastrophic claws in for the kill.

With a whip-like tail and devil horns,
The agonising pain of which it mourns,
Dagger-like teeth dig into your skin,
And takes you where the air is thin.

Breath of a ghost drifts across the air,
As the victim realises life isn't fair,
Hurt in the heart, like a bullet to the brain,
The family gathers in the pouring rain.

Catastrophic may well attack again,
The glow upon you now my dear friend,
So watch your back because here *it* comes,
It can hear the battle drums . . .

Alexandra Hunt, Rachel Spayne & Alexandra Hunt (13)
Sacred Heart RC School, Redcar

The Animal Of Light

Bathing in the moonlight
In the village below
Stood a mysterious creature,
That held an ominous glow.

Its shimmering sapphire eyes,
Which held and drew you in,
Seemed as pure as an angel's heart,
But were actually streaming with sin.

Because of the whiteness of its coat,
You would think it's sweet and kind,
But watch out for the ruby red bow,
Don't let it trick your mind.

Behind the suffocating mist,
The creature began to purr,
But as I edged closer,
Something strange started to occur.

The innocent feline vanished,
And the illusion became a reality,
Breath-taking things commenced
The air swamped with abnormality.

And what was left there,
Was a horrifying sight
Now ebony ugly creature,
Stood once where there was white.

Footsteps were heard
The feline retreated and retired
There was an eerie silence,
After two shocking shots were fired.

The flashing died out,
It laid in the dirt,
That poor, lifeless creature,
That they killed and hurt.

Megan McEwan, Heather Howes & Rebecca Doyle (13)
Sacred Heart RC School, Redcar

Communism Rage

Their rush for expansion,
And petty squabbles for land.
Natures of beliefs,
Their towering cities; empty of woodland.

Iron-willed in war,
'Heroic' says their memoirs.
Ascendancy is a boast.
Toting 'communism' as they toast.
Execution to the evil,
Then we'll travail the past.
Hungry for knowledge; the ghost prevails.
Extermination is the last.
Massacre, the only weep for the past.

Kevin Luke (14)
Sir Thomas Boughey Co-operative Business College, Newcastle under Lyme

Young Writers Information

We hope you have enjoyed reading this book - and that you will continue to enjoy it in the coming years.

If you like reading and writing poetry drop us a line, or give us a call, and we'll send you a free information pack.

Alternatively if you would like to order further copies of this book or any of our other titles, then please give us a call or log onto our website at www.youngwriters.co.uk

Young Writers Information
Remus House
Coltsfoot Drive
Peterborough
PE2 9JX

(01733) 890066